# Unit 1

***Have to, must, can't, and don't***

| | | | |
|---|---|---|---|
| We | **must** | come | to school on time. |
| | **have to** | | |

| | | | | |
|---|---|---|---|---|
| You | **can't (must not)** | throw | trash in the street. | *can't = can not* |
| | **Don't** | throw | trash in the street. | *don't = do not* |

To talk about rules, use *must, have to, can't,* and *don't.*

## 1 **Look and read.** Circle the correct answer.

1.  Everyone **has to** / **can't** pick up their trash.

2.  We **must** / **can't** recycle our bottles.

3.  People **have to** / **must not** fish in the river.

4.  You **must** / **can't** use your phone in the movie theater.

## 2 **Read and draw.**

1. You must not touch the sea turtles.

2. We have to recycle our trash.

3. Don't pollute the ocean!

## 3 **Read and write.** Use words from the box.

can't don't has to have to must must not

1. **We're at the beach.**

We have to protect sea life. ______ throw trash. ______ wear a bathing suit.

2. **He's at a restaurant.**

______ throw food. ______ choose his lunch. ______ bring his cat.

3. **They're at the zoo.**

______ see the dolphins. ______ miss the octopus. ______ touch the shark.

4. **You're at home.**

______ get up early for school. ______ go to bed after eleven o'clock. ______ make breakfast by myself.

## 4 **Read and write.** Answer the questions.

1. What must you do every day?

______

2. What do you have to do tomorrow?

______

3. What must you <u>not</u> do in school?

______

4. What can't you do before breakfast?

______

**Future with *will* and *won't***

| | | | | | |
|---|---|---|---|---|---|
| In the future, | we | **will** | know | more about the ocean floor. | *won't* = *will not* |
| | people | **won't** | drive | cars anymore. | |

| **Question** | | | | | **Answer** | |
|---|---|---|---|---|---|---|
| Where | **will** | we | live | in the future? | We**'ll** live in crowded cities. We **won't** live in small towns. | *we'll* = *we will* |
| | **Will** | people | live | longer? | Yes, they **will**. No, they **won't**. | |

When you aren't 100% sure, use *maybe*.
*In the future, will people live longer? / Maybe.*

## 1 **Read.** Circle the letter of the sentence that describes the future.

1. a. We are polluting the ocean, and it's hurting sea life.
   b. I won't pollute the ocean.
2. a. An oil spill will affect the animals in the ocean.
   b. Pollution affects sea life.
3. a. Will the children pick up the trash on the beach?
   b. Do you always recycle your plastic trash?
4. a. I want to live under the sea.
   b. People won't live under the sea.

## 2 **Unscramble.** Look at pp. 8–9 of your Student's Book.

1. top / will / near / the / of / the / dolphins / swim / ocean
   Dolphins will swim near the top of the ocean.
2. oil spills / sea / harm / will / life
   ______________________________
3. ocean's / creatures / middle layer / the / most / live / won't / in
   ______________________________
4. sunlight / won't / bottom / the / of / the / ocean / reach
   ______________________________

## 3 Read and write. Write about the future.

1. Robots will help (help) us with our work.
2. Tankers ________________ (not transport) oil across the ocean.
3. There ________________ (not be) trash in the sea in 100 years.
4. We ________________ (not use) plastic bottles or plastic bags.
5. People ________________ (take care of) the oceans better than they do now.

## 4 **Look at the Green Team's plan.** Answer the questions.

The Green Team will . . .

- ✓ clean up river banks.
- ✓ make "Keep It Clean" posters.
- ✓ invite people who live nearby to help.
- ✓ take bicycles not cars.
- ✓ camp in the park near the river.

1. What will the Green Team do next? They will clean up the river banks.
2. Will they clean the beaches? ________________
3. What will they write on their posters? ________________
4. Who will help them? ________________
5. Will they travel in cars? ________________
6. Where will they camp? ________________

## 5 **Write.** What are four things you'll do to protect the planet? Use *will* and *won't*.

________________

________________

________________

________________

# Unit 2

***Used to* for past habits**

| | | | | | |
|---|---|---|---|---|---|
| I | **used to** | play | outside. | These days | I play video games inside. |
| She | | | | | she plays video games inside. |
| Children | | | | | they play video games inside. |
| My friend | **didn't use to** | have | a computer. | Now | he has one. |

| Question | | | | | | Answer |
|---|---|---|---|---|---|---|
| Where | did | you | **use to** | play? | | I **used to** play in the park. |
| | Did | you | **use to** | play | in the park? | Yes, I did. / No, I didn't. |

*Used to* is different from *be* + *used to.*
*I used to do homework at night* = I did this regularly in the past, but not anymore.
*I am used to doing homework at night* = I do this regularly. It is not a problem for me.

## 1 **Read.** Circle the correct answer.

1. How did children **used to** / **use to** play?
2. People didn't **used to** / **use to** have computers.
3. People **used to** / **use to** watch TV in black and white.
4. Did your grandparents **used to** / **use to** have a black and white TV?

## 2 **Read and write.** Complete the conversations.

1. How ___did___ people ___use to wash___ (wash) their clothes?
   They ___didn't use to have___ (not have) washing machines.
   They ________________ (wash) their clothes by hand.
2. How ________________ people ________________ (take) a bath?
   They ________________ (not have) water in their houses.
3. ________________ children ________________ (learn) with computers at school?
   No, they ________________ (not learn) with computers at school.

## 3 **Look and write.** Complete the sentences about Jamie.

| | At six years old | Now |
|---|---|---|
| home | apartment | house |
| sport | soccer | basketball |
| favorite food | grapes | cookies |
| pet | hamster | dog |
| hobbies | color pictures | take photos |

1. Jamie used to live in an apartment. He didn't use to live in a house.
2. He ______________ color pictures. He ______________ take photos.
3. He ______________ a hamster. He ______________ a dog.
4. He ______________ soccer. He ______________ basketball.
5. His favorite food ______________ grapes. His favorite food ______________ cookies.

## 4 **Write.** Complete the chart like Jamie's. What used to be different for you? Choose categories and write sentences.

| | At six years old | Now |
|---|---|---|
| style | long hair | glasses |
| | | |
| | | |
| | | |
| | | |

I used to have long hair. I didn't use to wear glasses.

______________________________

______________________________

______________________________

______________________________

***You* for general statements**

| Question | | | | | Answer |
|---|---|---|---|---|---|
| What | can | you | do | on this computer? | **You** can play games and do homework. |
| How | do | | make | vegetable soup? | First, **you** wash the vegetables. Then **you** . . . |

*you* = people (in general)

## 1 **Rewrite the sentences.** Use *you* instead of the underlined words.

1. <u>People</u> should recycle more often.

   ______________________________

2. <u>All of the workers</u> must wear protective clothes.

   ______________________________

3. <u>Students</u> don't have to use scissors.

   ______________________________

4. <u>Families</u> can't feed the animals at the zoo.

   ______________________________

## 2 **Unscramble.** Circle the number for sentences that are *not* about people in general.

1. should / plastic / you / recycle

   ______________________________

2. my / help / bike / fix / you / me / can?

   ______________________________

3. drink / to / you / water / need

   ______________________________

4. scooter / should / a / you / new / get

   ______________________________

**3** **Look and write.** What do you use each item for? Write a sentence with *you*.

1.  ______________________________

2.  ______________________________

3.  ______________________________

4.  ______________________________

**4** **Draw an invention.** Answer the questions.

1. What is it? ______________________________
2. When do you use it? ______________________________
3. How do you use it? ______________________________
4. Why do you use it? ______________________________

**5** **Write.** Choose an object from the box. Explain how, when, and why you use it.

umbrella bicycle computer first-aid kit scissors stove

______________________________

______________________________

# Unit 3

**Describing people with *who***

| | |
|---|---|
| I have a classmate. | She likes math. |
| I have a classmate **who** likes math. | |
| Mateo has two friends. | They play basketball. |
| Mateo has two friends **who** play basketball. | |
| The girl is smart. | She sits next to me. |
| The girl **who** sits next to me is smart. | |
| The people are Canadian. | They live next door. |
| The people **who** live next door are Canadian. | |

You can use *who* in a sentence to give more information about people.

**1 Read.** Complete the sentences with *who* where it is necessary. If *who* isn't necessary, write *X*.

1. The children ______ play video games together like to compete.
2. The children ______ are competing in the contest.
3. The boy ______ knows how to play every video game well.
4. The boy ______ gave me this controller lives across the street.

**2 Read.** Rewrite as one sentence.

1. My brother is a good swimmer. He loves diving.

   My brother is a good swimmer who loves diving.

2. My mom is a baker. She makes delicious cakes.

   ______________________________

3. Abigail is a fast runner. She competes in sports.

   ______________________________

4. Bai is a student. He likes to take photos.

   ______________________________

## 3 **Write.** Write a sentence about each student's interests.

1. Akira / play video games

   Akira is the student who plays video games.

2. Rafa / enjoy taking care of animals

   ____________________

3. Kalinda / take beautiful photos

   ____________________

4. Jed / play baseball

   ____________________

5. Pablo / be good at math

   ____________________

## 4 **Write.** Complete the sentences. Use *who*.

1. A teacher is a person who helps students learn.
2. A doctor is someone ____________________
3. A basketball player is an athlete ____________________
4. My parents are people ____________________
5. My best friend is someone ____________________
6. Do you know a person ____________________

## 5 **Write.** Write about two people. Use *who* and a word in the box.

| be | collect | enjoy | help | listen | play | work |
|---|---|---|---|---|---|---|

My brother is a person who enjoys inventing things.

____________________

____________________

**Direct and indirect objects**

| | | | | | | |
|---|---|---|---|---|---|---|
| Sara | gave | **me** | the pencil. | | | Object pronouns: me, you, her, him, us, them |
| Sara | gave | | the pencil | **to** | **me**. | |
| My brother | made | **us** | breakfast. | | | |
| My brother | made | | breakfast | **for** | **us**. | |

The two sentences mean the same thing.

*Sara gave me the pencil.* = *Sara gave the pencil* ***to*** *me.*

With *make* and *buy*, use *for*: *Our teacher made / bought breakfast* ***for*** *us.*

## 1 **Read.** Match the sentences with the same meaning. Draw a line.

1. I showed my games to Nadia.
2. Nadia gave her games to me.
3. I sent two games to Beto and Nadia.
4. Beto sold some games to Nadia.
5. Beto sent some games to me and Nadia.
6. Nadia bought some games for Beto.

a. She bought him some games.
b. I sent them two games.
c. He sold her some games.
d. She gave me her games.
e. He sent us some games.
f. I showed her my games.

## 2 **Read.** Replace the underlined word(s).

1. My friends bought a dinosaur for Monica. (her)
2. She showed the photo to her friends.
3. I sent an e-mail to my brother.
4. We found some old comic books for Ana and Ivan.
5. The children made a cake for me and Katherine.
6. I played a video game with my sister.

## 3 **Rewrite the sentences.** Use *her, them,* and *us.*

1. Lea made Grandma a birthday card.

______________________________

2. Uncle Jon bought Clara and me some presents.

______________________________

3. Bela gave the scientists the fossils she found.

______________________________

## 4 **Write.** Rewrite each sentence from Activity 3. Use *to* or *for.*

1. ______________________________
2. ______________________________
3. ______________________________

## 5 **Read and write.** Answer the questions.

1. What did your friend give you for your birthday?

My friend gave me a book for my birthday.

2. What clothing did your mom buy for you before school started?

______________________________

3. What object did a teacher show students in your class this week?

______________________________

4. What did you make for someone in your family?

______________________________

5. Who did you send an important e-mail to this month?

______________________________

# Unit 4

## Cause and effect with double comparatives

| | | | |
|---|---|---|---|
| **The more** | she reads, | **the more** | she learns. |
| **The more** | I think about the problem, | **the more** | I worry about it. |
| **The more** | you push the swing, | **the higher** | it goes. |
| **The more** | we practice English, | **the better** | we will speak. |

In each sentence, the first action causes the second action.

***The more** she reads*, ***the more** she learns*.

first action second action

You can also use *will* with the second action.

*The more she reads, the more she will learn.*

## 1 **Read and match.** Draw a line.

1. The faster you pedal,
2. The harder I push my foot down,
3. The earlier you get up,
4. The more time they spend in the park,
5. The less I eat,

a. the more you can do in the morning.
b. the faster you'll get to school.
c. the hungrier I am.
d. the more fun they will have.
e. the faster my scooter goes.

## 2 **Read.** Check T for *True* and F for *False*. Then correct the false answers.

1. The ~~slower~~ faster she spins, the more difficult it is to stop. (T) (F) ✓
2. The less sugar you eat, the worse your teeth will be. (T) (F)
3. The earlier you go to bed, the less tired you will feel. (T) (F)
4. The less he pushes his friend, the higher he will go. (T) (F)
5. The more we stretch our muscles, the worse we will run. (T) (F)
6. The more force you use, the higher the ball goes. (T) (F)

## 3 **Read and write.** Complete the sentences with a word from the box.

better cleaner faster harder ~~higher~~ worse

1. The stronger the wind, the higher the kite will go.
2. The less you practice, the __________ it is to win.
3. The dizzier she gets, the __________ she feels.
4. The more he pedals, the __________ he goes.
5. The less plastic we use, the __________ our oceans will be.
6. The more fruit you eat, the __________ you will feel.

## 4 **Read and write.** Complete the sentences.

1. The more water a flower gets, __________.
2. The less I talk, __________.
3. The more vegetables children eat, __________.
4. The longer my friends and I play outside, __________.

## 5 **Write.** Write about your own activities. Use the words in the box.

| | |
|---|---|
| better | less |
| earlier | longer |
| faster | more |
| harder | sooner |
| later | worse |

The more I watch TV, the less I study.

__________

__________

__________

__________

**Definitions with *which***

| | |
|---|---|
| Gravity is a force. | It pulls you toward Earth. |
| Gravity is a force **which** pulls you toward Earth. | |
| A carnivore is an animal. | It eats meat. |
| A carnivore is an animal **which** eats meat. | |
| Skates are special shoes. | You wear them on the ice. |
| Skates are special shoes **which** you wear on the ice. | |
| Honey is a sweet food. | Bees make it. |
| Honey is a sweet food **which** bees make. | |

You can use *which* to combine sentences.

## 1 **Read.** Write *which* when necessary. If it's not necessary, write *X*.

1. Gravity ________________ pulls you toward the center of the earth.
2. Gravity is the force ________________ holds everything in place.
3. Tennis is a sport ________________ needs two or four people.
4. I play tennis ________________ with three of my school friends.
5. Pedaling ________________ makes a bicycle move.

## 2 **Write.** Use *which* and the words provided.

1. ice cream / sweet food / eat when it's hot outside.

   Ice cream is a sweet food which you eat when it's hot outside.
2. markers / tools / use to color pictures

   ________________________________________
3. basketball / sport / play with an orange ball

   ________________________________________
4. butterfly / insect / have beautiful wings

   ________________________________________
5. swing / object / move forward and backward

   ________________________________________

## 3 **Write.** Complete the sentences using *which*.

1. A computer is an invention which we use all the time.
2. ______ is an object ______.
3. ______ is a language ______.
4. ______ is a sport ______.
5. ______ is a game ______.
6. ______ is a fruit ______.

## 4 **Look and write.** Describe each object using *which*.

1. 

A toothbrush is something which you use to clean your teeth.

2. 

______

3. 

______

4. 

______

## 5 **Write.** Choose an object in your classroom. Write three clues to describe it. Use *which*.

______

______

# Unit 5

### Future predictions and plans with *be going to*

| | | | | |
|---|---|---|---|---|
| It'**s** | **going to** | rain | tomorrow. | *It's = It is*<br>*I'm = I am*<br>*They're = They are* |
| I'**m** | | call | my friend. | |
| They'**re** | | play | basketball. | |

| **Question** | | | | | | **Answer** |
|---|---|---|---|---|---|---|
| | **Is** | it | **going to** | rain | tomorrow? | Yes, it is.<br>No, it isn't. |
| What | **are** | they | | do | | They'**re going to** play basketball. |

Use *be going to* to talk about the future.

**1** **Read.** Complete the sentences.

1. We just saw lightning. Next there 's going to be thunder.
2. A sandstorm is coming. My parents ________ get the house ready.
3. It's snowing. He ________ wear a warm coat.
4. It's hot today. I ________ go swimming.

**2** **Read and write.** Answer the questions. Use *going to* and phrases from the box.

bring an umbrella | close all the windows | evacuate | ~~make a snowman~~

1. What are you going to do in the snow?
   I'm going to make a snowman.
2. What are you going to do if it's rainy?
   ________
3. How is your family going to get ready for the sandstorm?
   ________
4. What are your cousins going to do if there's a flood?
   ________

**3** **Read and write.** Read about what's happening today. Then say that tomorrow things are going to be different.

1. Today it's really cold.

   Tomorrow it's going to be hot.
2. Today I'm getting up early.

   ______
3. Today my brother is staying home.

   ______
4. Today my parents aren't working.

   ______
5. Today it's raining.

   ______

**4** **Read and write.** Answer with information that is true for you.

1. Is it going to rain much this week where you live?

   No, but it's going to be cloudy.
2. What are you not going to do if there's thunder and lightning?

   ______
3. What are you going to do if there's a flood?

   ______
4. If you have to evacuate your house, where are you going to go?

   ______

**5** **Write.** There's no school because of a blizzard. Write four things you're going to do today.

______

______

______

______

**Zero conditional (present tense)**

| | | | | | | |
|---|---|---|---|---|---|---|
| If | it | **snows,** | | school | **starts** | late. |
| | it | **is** | raining, | I | **use** | an umbrella. |
| | I | **go to bed** | late, | I | **am** | tired the next day. |

These two sentences mean the same thing. In sentence 1, notice the comma.
*If it snows, school starts late.*
*School starts late if it snows.*

## 1 **Read.** Circle the correct answer.

1. **If there** / **There's** is an emergency, we follow our plan.
2. If it rains, then **if I use** / **I use** an umbrella.
3. If a tornado comes, **if we evacuate** / **we evacuate**.
4. If Jon knows it's going to be cold, he **wears** / **wore** his coat and gloves.
5. **Is** / **If** it's hot, we go swimming.
6. If **there** / **there's** a blizzard, we don't have school.

## 2 **Read and write.** Complete the sentences.

1. If it's hurricane season, it rains a lot.
2. If it snows, __________
3. If the electricity goes out, __________
4. If a blizzard comes, __________
5. If there's no rain for weeks, __________
6. If there's a flood in my town, __________

## 3 **Read and write.** Complete the sentences with a phrase beginning with *if*.

1. If there's a blizzard_______________, people can't drive.
2. ______________________________, we need a flashlight.
3. ______________________________, I make an emergency plan.
4. ______________________________, I call my parents.
5. ______________________________, people evacuate.
6. ______________________________, we go to a storm shelter.

## 4 **Read and write.** Answer the questions in complete sentences.

1. What do people wear if it rains?

   If it rains, people wear rain boots.

2. What do you do if it snows?

   ______________________________

3. What does your family do if a tornado comes?

   ______________________________

4. What do people do if there is a drought?

   ______________________________

## 5 **Write.** Write five sentences using the phrases in the box and *if*.

| | | |
|---|---|---|
| be very windy | feel cold | hear about a tornado on the radio |
| miss the bus | ~~see a lion~~ | see thunder and lightning |

If I see a lion, I run.

______________________________

______________________________

______________________________

______________________________

______________________________

# Unit 6

**Comparisons with *as . . . as***

| | | | | | |
|---|---|---|---|---|---|
| The frog | is | **as** | big | **as** | my hand. |
| Lions | are**n't** | | fast | | cheetahs. |

*as . . . as* = The two things are the same.
*not as . . . as* = The two things are different.

**1** **Read.** Circle the correct answer.

1. A cheetah is **faster than** / **as fast as** an elephant.
2. An elephant is **larger than** / **as large as** a horse.
3. A poisonous spider is **more dangerous than** / **as dangerous as** a non-poisonous spider.
4. Zebras are about **as big as** / **much bigger than** horses.
5. A bee is **smaller than** / **as small as** a salamander.

**2** **Read and write.** Compare using *as . . . as* and the words in parentheses.

1. A deer is not ____________________ (fast) a jaguar.
2. Otters can be ____________________ (playful) monkeys.
3. Some frogs are ____________________ (poisonous) snakes.
4. Donkeys are not ____________________ (beautiful) horses.
5. A cat is not ____________________ (loud) a lion.
6. An alligator's skin is not ____________________ (smooth) a seal's skin.

## 3 **Read and write.** Compare using *(not) as . . . as.*

1. A bee's sting can be dangerous, but a poisonous spider's bite is more dangerous!

   A bee's sting is not as dangerous as a poisonous spider's bite.
2. My sister thinks baby seals are really cute. She thinks lion cubs are really cute, too!

   ______________________________
3. Cheetahs can run at a speed of around 110 kph (68 mph). Sailfish can swim 110 kph.

   ______________________________
4. A baby elephant is big! It weighs about 90 kg (200 lb.), the same as two small people.

   ______________________________

## 4 **Write.** Compare using *(not) as . . . as.*

1. insect / leaf

   Some insects are as green as a leaf.
2. cat's fur / rabbit's fur

   ______________________________
3. seal / elephant

   ______________________________
4. snakes / crocodiles

   ______________________________
5. baby seal / baby otter

   ______________________________

## 5 **Write.** Write five sentences comparing yourself to people just like you.

I am as old as my cousin Jack.

______________________________

______________________________

______________________________

______________________________

______________________________

## Tag questions

| Positive | | | Negative | |
|---|---|---|---|---|
| The tiger | **is** | beautiful, | **isn't** | it? |
| Rabbits | **are** | fast, | **aren't** | they? |
| The lion | **was** | loud, | **wasn't** | it? |
| Dinosaurs | **were** | everywhere, | **weren't** | they? |
| | | | | |
| You | **eat** | bread, | **don't** | you? |
| A spider | **eats** | insects, | **doesn't** | it? |
| The turtles | **ate** | the fish, | **didn't** | they? |

| Negative | | | Positive | |
|---|---|---|---|---|
| This snake | **isn't** | poisonous, | **is** | it? |
| You | **aren't** | afraid of bees, | **are** | you? |
| That fish | **wasn't** | dangerous, | **was** | it? |
| Those | **weren't** | ants, | **were** | they? |
| | | | | |
| You | **don't** eat | bread, | **do** | you? |
| A spider | **doesn't** eat | plants, | **does** | it? |
| The turtles | **didn't** eat | the fish, | **did** | they? |

Use a pronoun at the end of the sentence.
*The tiger is beautiful, isn't it?*
*Rabbits are fast, aren't they?*

## 1 **Read.** Circle the letter.

1. Some species look like others, ______?
   a. do they  b. don't they  c. aren't they
2. Copycat animals are amazing, ______?
   a. isn't they  b. don't they  c. aren't they
3. Those deer weren't running from a lion, ______?
   a. were they  b. aren't they  c. weren't they
4. Donkeys are funny animals, ______?
   a. can't they  b. aren't they  c. are they

## 2 **Read and write.** Complete the questions.

1. Some insects are poisonous, ______________?
2. Camouflage doesn't help all animals hide, ______________?
3. Those fish swim fast, ______________?
4. That frog had stripes, ______________?
5. A cheetah can run faster than a human, ______________?
6. The dog we saw yesterday wasn't very nice, ______________?

## 3 **Look and write.** Ask a question about each animal.

1.  *This butterfly is beautiful, isn't it?*

2.  ______________________________

3.  ______________________________

4.  ______________________________

5.  ______________________________

6.  ______________________________

## 4 **Write.** Write four questions to ask your friend about this week's events.

*The game we played after school was fun, wasn't it?*

______________________________

______________________________

______________________________

______________________________

# Unit 7

**Present perfect with *ever* and *never***

| Question | | | | | Answer | |
|---|---|---|---|---|---|---|
| **Have** | you | ever | **played** | the drums? | Yes, I **have**.<br>Yes, I**'ve played** them many times. | *I've = I have*<br>*haven't = have not* |
| | | | | | No, I **haven't**.<br>No, I**'ve** never **played** the drums. | |
| **Has** | he | ever | **heard** | that song? | Yes, he **has**.<br>Yes, he**'s heard** that song twice. | *he's = he has*<br>*hasn't = has not* |
| | | | | | No, he **hasn't**.<br>No, he**'s** never **heard** that song. | |

*twice* = two times
*never* = at no time in the past

## 1 **Read and match.** Draw a line.

1. Has she ever sung in a band?
2. Have you ever danced at a concert?
3. Have they ever played music together?
4. Has he seen his favorite band play?
5. Have we ever been in band class together?

a. No, I never have.
b. Yes, she has.
c. No, we never have.
d. Yes, they have.
e. No, he never has.

## 2 **Read.** Complete the sentences with *ever* or *never*.

1. I have ___never___ played this instrument before.
2. I have __________ seen your violin before.
3. This will be the first time I have __________ played that song.
4. Have you __________ been in an orchestra?
5. My parents have __________ heard this band play.
6. I have __________ felt both so nervous and so excited before.
7. Have you __________ seen such unusual instruments?
8. No, we __________ have.

**3** **Read and write.** Answer the questions in complete sentences.

1. Have you ever played the saxophone?

   No, I have never played the saxophone.

2. Have you ever had guitar lessons?

3. Have you ever written a song?

4. Have your friends ever heard you sing?

5. Have you ever met a famous musician? If so, who?

**4** **Write.** Write questions with the words. Then answer them in complete sentences.

1. flute

   Have you ever played flute?

   Yes, I have played the flute.

2. drums

3. concert

4. lead singer

**5** **Write.** Write two interesting things you have done. Write two things you have never done.

I have seen a Chinese opera.

**Comparative adverbs**

<table>
<tr><td rowspan="2">She</td><td>sleeps</td><td>longer</td><td colspan="2" rowspan="2">than</td><td rowspan="4">I do.</td></tr>
<tr><td>plays</td><td>better</td></tr>
<tr><td rowspan="2">He</td><td>sings</td><td rowspan="2">more</td><td>beautifully</td><td rowspan="2">than</td></tr>
<tr><td>practices</td><td>often</td></tr>
</table>

<table>
<tr><td rowspan="2">She</td><td>sleeps</td><td rowspan="4">as</td><td>long</td><td rowspan="4">as</td><td rowspan="4">I do.</td></tr>
<tr><td>plays</td><td>well</td></tr>
<tr><td rowspan="2">He</td><td>sings</td><td>beautifully</td></tr>
<tr><td>practices</td><td>often</td></tr>
</table>

Irregular forms: *well* → *better (than)* *badly* → *worse (than)*
With *often*, you can use *more* or *less*: *He practices* *<u>more often</u>* */ <u>less often</u> than I do.*

## 1 **Read.** Circle the correct answer.

1. I like pop music **more well** / **better** than I like rock.
2. He can't sing very well. He sings **worse** / **less better** than I do.
3. Like me, my sister practices piano every day. She practices **harder** / **as hard as** I do.
4. My dad sings **more loudly** / **as loudly** than anyone else in the family.
5. When he dances, his feet move **faster than** / **less fast** mine.
6. She plays piano on Sundays, but I play every day. She plays **better** / **less often** than I do.

## 2 **Write.** Complete the sentences.

1. I like being in the jazz band ___as well as___ (=, well) being in the orchestra.
2. She can play the violin ______________ (+, well) she can play the piano.
3. He listens to classical music ______________ (-, often) he listens to rock.
4. Do you sing ______________ (=, badly) your sister?
5. When my dad plays guitar, his hands move ______________ (+, fast) mine do.
6. He plays the guitar ______________ (=, often) he plays the drums.

## 3 **Write.** Use the words to write comparative sentences.

1. he / sing / =, well / sister

   He sings as well as his sister (does).

2. she / practice piano / -, often / brother

3. she / play flute / +, beautifully / her teacher

4. he / listen to rock music / +, often / his friend

5. musicians / play / drums / +, loudly / violin

6. I / dance ballet / =, well / hip-hop

## 4 **Read and write.** Answer the questions using comparatives.

1. What do you listen to more often—rock or hip-hop?

   I listen to hip-hop more often than I listen to rock.

2. Who sings better—you or your best friend?

3. What do you do as well as your parents?

4. What do you play more often—sports or music?

5. Think of your two favorite bands. Which one do you like better?

# Unit 8

***May* and *might***

| | | | | |
|---|---|---|---|---|
| There | **may** **might** | (not) | be | life in our solar system outside Earth. |
| We | | | receive | messages from extraterrestrials in the future. |

You can use *may* and *might* to talk about the present or the future. They mean the same thing.

## 1 **Read and match.** Draw a line.

1. What star is that?
2. Is there life on other planets?
3. What was that shape moving in the sky?
4. Will extraterrestrials visit Earth?

a. There might be.
b. It may be the North Star.
c. They may.
d. I thought it might be a comet.

## 2 **Read and write.** Complete the sentences with *may* or *might*.

1. We think Jupiter ___may/might___ have moons that we haven't discovered yet.
2. I think other solar systems ________________ also have planets like Earth.
3. Someday people ________________ be able to go to space on vacation.
4. The astronauts ________________ have to be in space for many months.
5. He ________________ go to space camp someday.
6. She didn't agree that there ________________ be life in other galaxies.
7. They knew that the big star in the sky ________________ actually be a planet.
8. Have you heard there ________________ be a new planet in our solar system?

## 3 **Read and write.** Use words from the box and *may* or *might*.

| | | | | | |
|---|---|---|---|---|---|
| be | come | have | see | ~~try~~ | win |

1. They thought extraterrestrials __might try__ to contact us.
2. Scientists say that a comet ________________ close to Earth in a few years.
3. We thought that the movie about life on other planets ________________ the prize for best film.
4. There ________________ more galaxies than we know in the universe.
5. We thought scientists ________________ water on Mars.

## 4 **Read and write.** Answer the questions with your own ideas. Use *may* or *might*.

1. Is there a planet that doesn't have a moon?

   There might be a planet that doesn't have a moon.
2. How long will it take to receive a message from extraterrestrials?

   ________________________________
3. When will we next see a comet in the sky?

   ________________________________
4. Do plants and animals live on other planets?

   ________________________________
5. How many galaxies are there?

   ________________________________

## 5 **Look and write.** Imagine this is a new planet. Write three sentences about it. Use *may* or *might*.

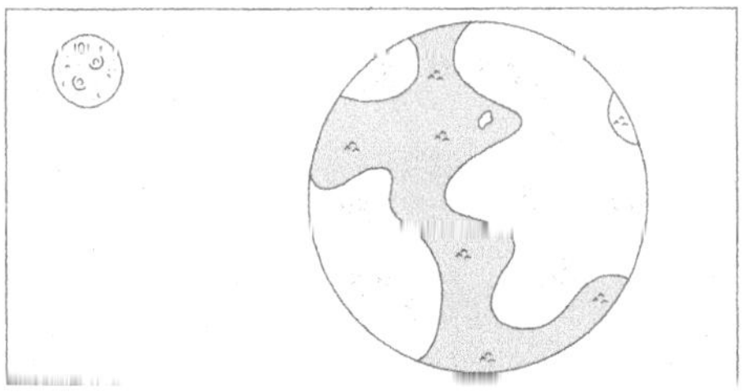

There might be trees on this planet.

________________________________

________________________________

________________________________

**Indefinite pronouns**

**Everyone** in this class works hard. We all work hard.

**Someone** ate my apple, but I don't know who.

I don't think **anyone** wants to live on the moon.
Does **anyone** want to live on the moon?

**No one** was late to school yesterday. **Everyone** was on time.

Use *anyone* in negative sentences and questions.
*I don't think **anyone** wants to live on the moon.* (Not: ~~*I don't think **no one** wants to live on the moon.*~~)
*Does **anyone** want to live on the moon?* (Not: ~~*Does **someone** want to live on the moon?*~~)

**1** **Read.** Match the word that can replace each underlined phrase. Draw a line.

1. Each kid in my class wants to fly to the moon. — a. no one
2. Did you talk to any of the astronauts who visited school? — b. everyone
3. My phone is ringing. Another person is trying to call me. — c. anyone
4. Nobody who lives here is home. — d. someone

**2** **Read.** Circle the correct answer.

1. Outer space is really interesting! **Everyone** / **No one** is interested in space, aren't they?
2. **No one** / **Someone** from another planet might try to communicate with us. Don't be surprised if you hear about it someday.
3. Most people don't believe there's life on other planets. Does **everyone** / **anyone** think extraterrestrials are out there?
4. I want to believe in extraterrestrials, but really there's **no one** / **anyone** out there.
5. We were all invited to see the stars with a scientist. I'd like **no one** / **everyone** in the group to go.
6. **Someone** / **Anyone** is coming to speak to our class. I think it might be an astronomer.

**3** **Read and write.** Complete the paragraph. Use *anyone, everyone, no one,* and *someone.*

Not ________________ says that there is life on other planets. Do you think ________________ is out there that's as smart as humans? Some people say there's ________________ out there at all. Others definitely say that there's life on other planets. Do you know ________________ who says they have seen an extraterrestrial? I want to say that ________________ is out there, but I might not really believe ________________ who said they saw an extraterrestrial.

**4** **Read and write.** Rewrite the sentences. Use *anyone, everyone, no one,* and *someone.*

1. All the kids in my class went to the science center.
   Everyone went to the science center.
2. The teacher asked if any of the students knew all the planets.
   ________________
3. One student could name all of them.
   ________________
4. I knew that none of the students could name the comets.
   ________________
5. We all learned a lot about our solar system.
   ________________

**5** **Look and write.** Write three questions and answers. Use *anyone, everyone, no one,* and *someone.*

Is anyone playing the violin? No, no one is playing the violin.

________________

________________

________________